High Voice

Daffodils, Violets & Snowflakes

24 Classical Songs for Young Women Ages Ten to Mid-Teens

Compiled by Joan Frey Boytim

ISBN 978-0-634-06181-3

7777 W. BLUEMOUND RD. P.O. BOX 13819 MILWAUKEE, WI 53213

In Australia Contact:
Hal Leonard Australia Pty. Ltd.
4 Lentara Court
Cheltenham, Victoria, 3192 Australia
Email: ausadmin@halleonard.com.au

Visit Hal Leonard Online at
www.halleonard.com

PREFACE

Daffodils, Violets & Snowflakes is a supplementary classical solo book compiled for the enjoyment of late elementary, junior high and middle school girls. The high and low volumes each contain the same twenty-four songs, with companion accompaniments recorded by Laura Ward for those who use these learning aids.

This book is not intended to be the primary "first" book of songs; however, it can complement the *36 Solos for Young Singers* and the *Easy Songs for the Beginning Soprano* and *Easy Songs for the Beginning Mezzo-Soprano/Alto*. The songs are mostly previously out of print material which is unfamiliar but is suitable for the student with an imaginative mind and a flair for storytelling in songs such as "Daddy's Sweetheart," "Four and Twenty Snowflakes," and "Ho! Mr. Piper." Some of the songs are particularly good for playing different characters in a singing dialogue, such as "The Leaves and the Wind," "Nursery Rhymes," "To My First Love," and "You'd Better Ask Me." As the book title suggests, most of the songs relate to subjects of nature, love, flowers, birds, or the seasons.

Even though there are some short, very easy songs, there are quite a number of challenging selections for the musically talented and ambitious girls in your studio. Some of the ranges are a bit extended, but include optional notes for those students who require a limited range. Several of the songs introduce the florid style of singing with short, gentle moving passages. Many of the songs could be termed "encore" style songs, having a humorous touch to them.

In addition, women looking for solo pieces that would be particularly attractive to selected audiences, especially of young people, may find that there are many possibilities for grouping three or four songs together as "theme" sets for performance purposes.

The main intent is to provide a collection of songs that are fun to sing and still have a musicianship development component.

Joan Frey Boytim
May, 2003

CONTENTS

BOATS OF MINE

Robert Louis Stevenson

Anne Stratton Miller

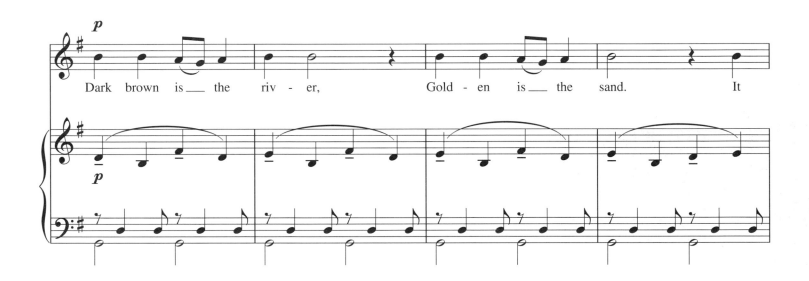

Dark brown is the riv - er, Gold - en is the sand. It

flows a - long for ev - er, With trees on ei - ther hand.

hun - dred miles or more, Oth - er lit - tle

chil - dren Shall bring my boats a - shore,

Shall bring my boats a shore.

CARE FLIES FROM THE LAD THAT IS MERRY

Garrick's Cymon

Michael Arne
Realization by Percy E. Fletcher

Care flies___ from the lad that is mer-ry, Whose___ heart is as sound and

cheeks are as round, Whose heart is as sound and___ cheeks are as round, As___

heart is as sound and cheeks are as round, As round and as

red, as red as a cher - ry, Whose

cresc. heart is as sound and__ cheeks are as round, As__ round and as red__ as a

cher - ry.

AN APRIL GIRL

Mary Mapes Dodge

J. Remington Fairlamb

* a speck in the air that is visible in sun ray

DADDY'S SWEETHEART

Curtis Hardin-Burnley
(Adapted)

Liza Lehmann

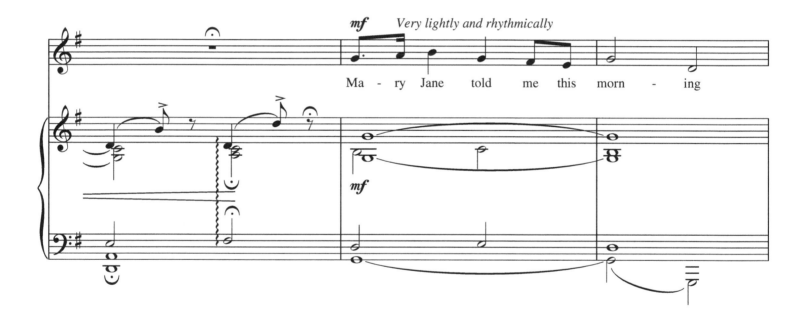

Oh, if moth-er had-n't mar-ried Dad-dy, Dad-dy might have mar-ried

me!

p con tenerezza

Of-ten he calls me his

p dolce

"Sweet — heart," He loves me such a lot! If

cresc.

THE LINNET'S SECRET

Dorothy Cook

Alec Rowley

told it to the Breeze, Who told the Lin - net's se - cret to the

Star - lings in the trees.

The Star - lings told a Wea - zel, and the

Wea - zel went to see What the se - cret that was hid - den 'neath the

DOES HE LOVE ME, OR LOVE ME NOT?

Music and Words by
ANDREW STERLING

1. A maid, young and fair, strayed
2. The pet - als were fall - ing

one bright day. Where the dai - sies and but - ter - cups grew,_____
one by one, As the ques - tions she asked o'er and o'er,_____

heart faith - ful be? Does he sigh for me? Or, re - joice that I'm far a -
flow'r blush to tell what it knew so well That she wor - ship'd a love un -

REFRAIN
molto espressivo

way?" "Does he love me or love me not?
true?

mf

Tell me, O sim - ple flow'r, Has his heart all its

vows for - got? Tho' I think of him ev' - ry hour?

THE FAIRY PIPERS

Fred E. Weatherly

A. Herbert Brewer

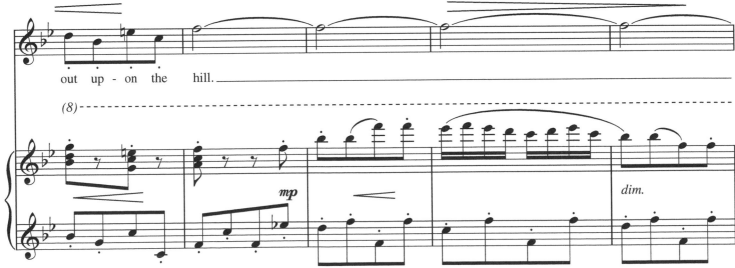

Come out! come out! Lis - ten on the air!

Up there! down there! Play - ing ev - 'ry - where! Oh hark! Oh

hear! Don't you hear the tune? Air - y fair - y pip - ers un - der -

neath the mer - ry moon!

They'll play to you of Cu - pid's tricks, Of love - ly queens and kings, Of fights and fun and pol - i - tics And lots of oth - er things.

Oh hark! Oh hear! Can't you hear them

FOUR AND TWENTY SNOWFLAKES

Music and Words by
William Stickles

Allegretto

Four and twen-ty snow-flakes came tumb-ling from the sky, and said:

"Let us make a snow-drift we can if we but try." So

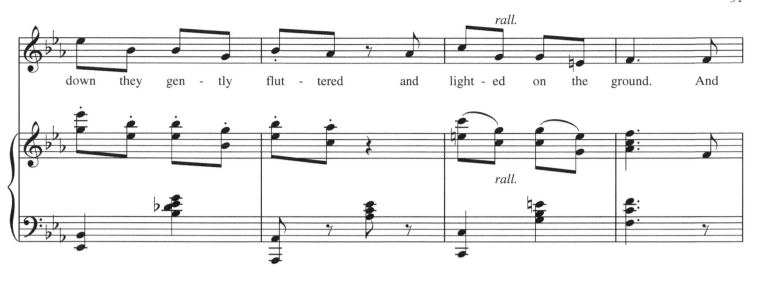

down they gen - tly flut - tered and light - ed on the ground. And

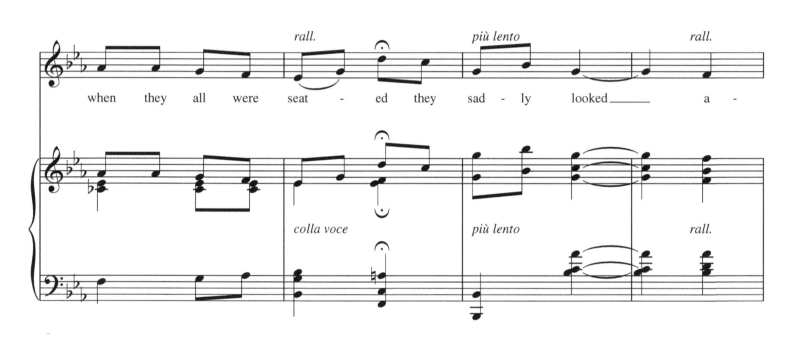

when they all were seat - ed they sad - ly looked_____ a -

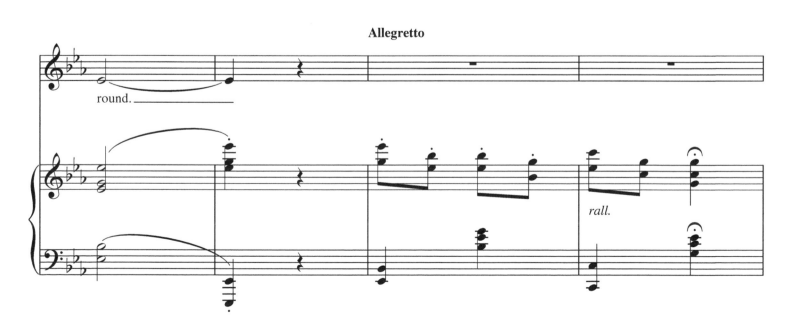

round._____

Allegretto

"We're ver - y few, in - deed," sighed they, "and we

a tempo

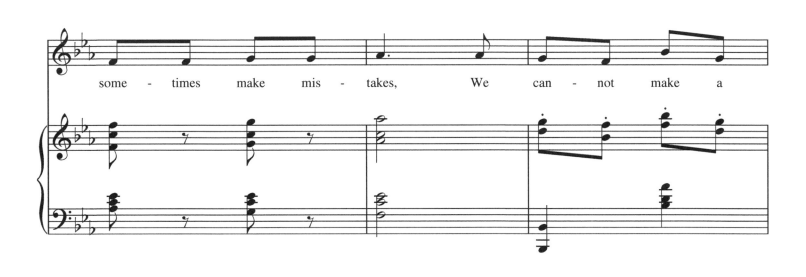

some - times make mis - takes, We can - not make a

snow - drift with four and twen - ty flakes." Just

rall.

a tempo

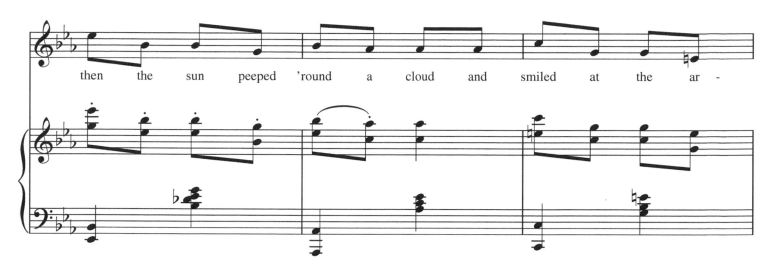

then the sun peeped 'round a cloud and smiled at the ar -

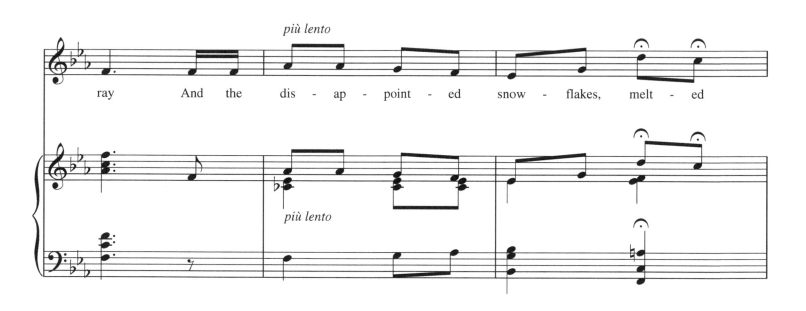

ray And the dis - ap - point - ed snow - flakes, melt - ed

più lento

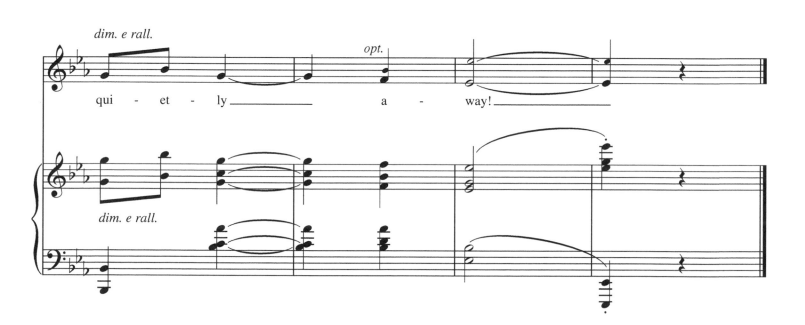

dim. e rall.

qui - et - ly_____ a - way!_____

opt.

HEIGH-HO! THE SUNSHINE

Ancie B. Marsland

Montague F. Phillips

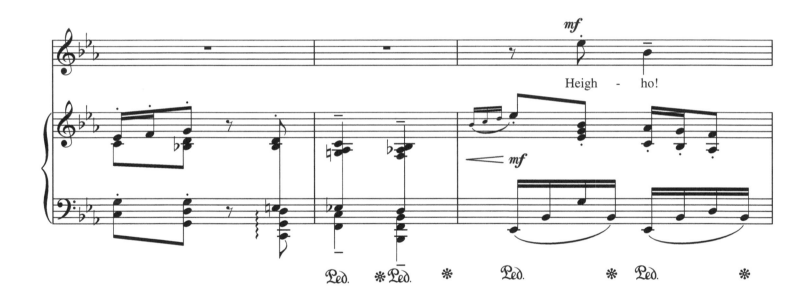

Heigh - ho!

where - fore sigh? Love is last - ing, time will fly:____

All thy days of ___ lone - ly pain Go, when love comes ___

back a - gain. Smile, and sing my ___ glad re - frain ___

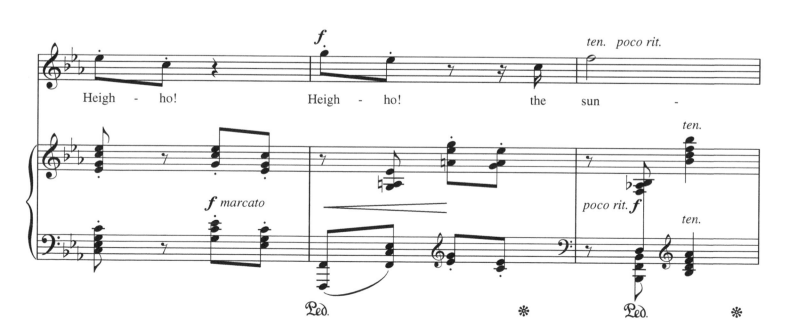

Heigh - ho! Heigh - ho! the sun -

shine.

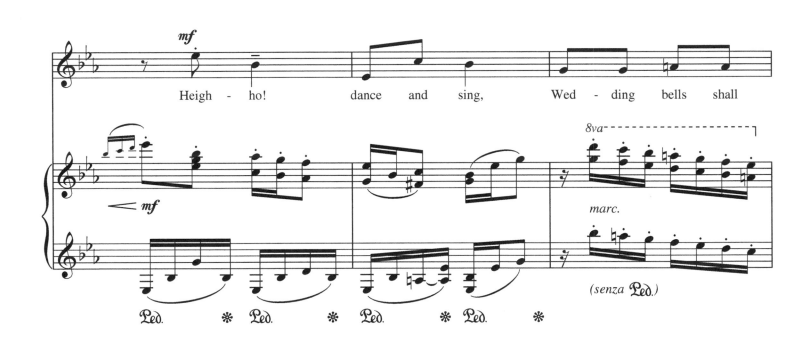

Heigh - ho! dance and sing, Wed - ding bells shall

sure - ly___ ring:_____ Love's re - turn will__ be ere long,

HER DREAM

Walter S. Poague

Frank Waller

"Do you be - lieve in dreams?" said he, "Of

course I do," said she, "For you're a dream to me, And

I be - lieve in you." He up and kissed her then, For

that's the way with men, And she just mur - mured

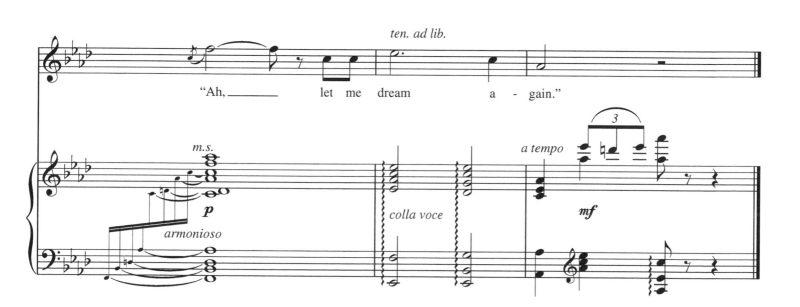

"Ah, let me dream a - gain."

HO! MR. PIPER

Music and Words by
Pearl G. Curran

poco rit. *opt.*
a tempo

run - ning far too fast! Ah! Ha!

poco rit. *ff*
a tempo
Ped. ✱

Ha!! *ten.* *tr*
f

(with surprise) *rit.*
O! Mis - ter Pi - per, I did - n't think they'd hear:
ff *p* *p colla voce*

(with regret)
All the dain - ty lit - tle things be - gin to dis - ap - pear;

KITTY OF COLERAINE

Irish Folksong
Arr. Joan Frey Boytim

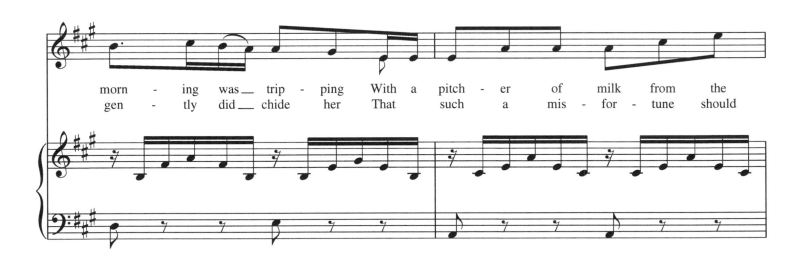

pitch - er it tum - bled, And all the sweet but - ter - milk wat - er'd the plain. "Oh!__
ere I did lave her She vow'd for such pleas - ure she'd break it a - gain. 'Twas__

what shall I do now? 'Twas look - ing at you, now; Sure, sure, such a pitch - er I'll
hay - mak - ing sea - son, I can't tell the rea - son Mis - for - tune will nev - er come

ne'er meet a - gain; 'Twas the pride of my dai - ry, Oh! Bar - ney Mc - Clea - ry, You're
sin - gle, 'tis plain, For__ ver - y soon af - ter poor Kit - ty's dis - ast - er There

sent as a plague to the girls of Cole - raine."
was not a pitch - er found whole in Cole - raine.

THE LEAVES AND THE WIND

George Cooper

Franco Leoni

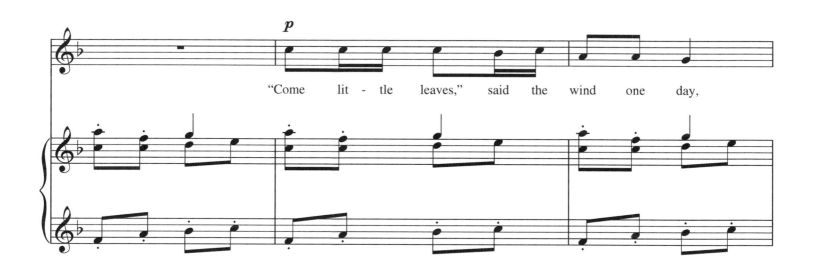

"Come lit - tle leaves," said the wind one day,

"Come o'er the mead - ows with me and play; Put on your dress - es of

red and gold, Sum - mer is gone, and the days grow cold."

Soon as the leaves heard the wind's loud call, Down they came flut - ter - ing

one and all; O - ver the brown fields they

danc'd and flew, _____ Sing - ing the

LITTLE MAID OF ARCADEE

from *Thespis*

W.S. Gilbert

Arthur Sullivan

Hap - py lit - tle maid - en she, Hap - py maid of Ar - ca - dee! Hap - py maid of Ar - ca - dee!

Mo - ments sped as mo - ments will, Rap - id - ly e -

nough; un - til Af - ter, say, a month or two, Rob - in did as Rob - ins do,

Fick - le as the month of May, Jilt - ed her and ran a - way!

Wretch - ed lit - tle maid - en she! Dole - ful maid of Ar - ca - dee! Dole - ful maid of Ar - ca - dee!

MOLLY MALONE

Irish Folksong
Arr. by W. Rhys-Herbert

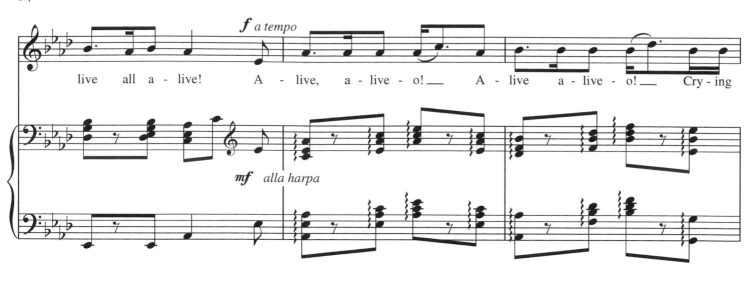

live all a - live! A - live, a - live - o!__ A - live a - live - o!__ Cry - ing

"Cock - les and mus - sels, a - live, all a - live!"

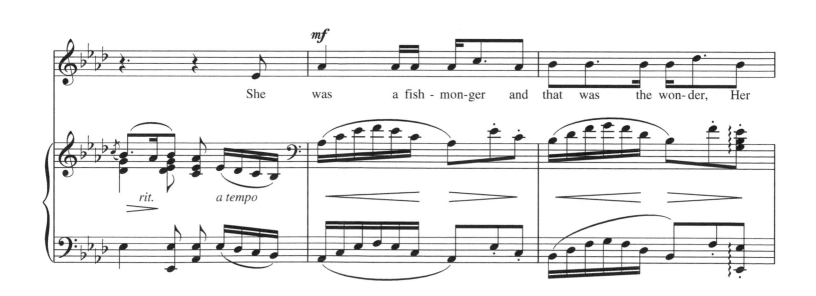

She was a fish - mon - ger and that was the won - der, Her

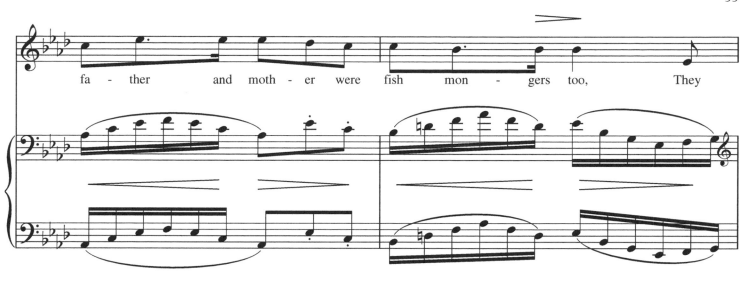

father and moth-er were fish mon - gers too, They

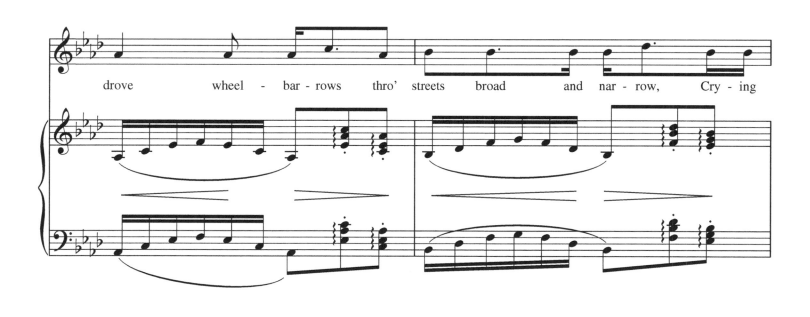

drove wheel - bar - rows thro' streets broad and nar - row, Cry - ing

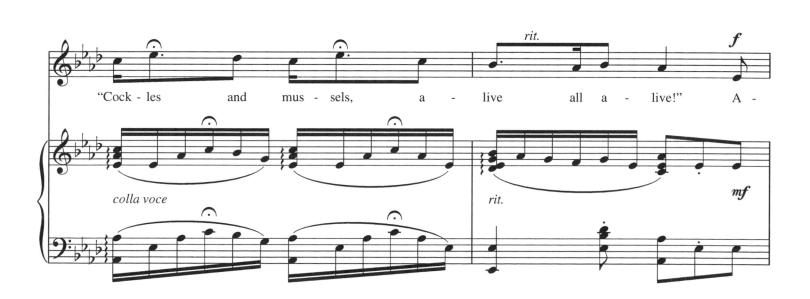

"Cock - les and mus - sels, a - live all a - live!" A -

a tempo

alla harpa

live, a - live - o! ___ A - live, a - live - o! ___ Cry - ing

rit.

"Cock - les and mus - sels, a - live all a - live!"

rit.

Slower

She

pp Much slower

pp Much slower

died of the fa - vor,* and noth - ing could save her, And

*fever

THE MINUET

Mary Mapes Dodge

Joseph Mosenthal

1. Grand - ma told me all a - bout it, Told me, so I could - n't
2. Grand - ma's hair was bright and sun - ny; Dim - pled cheeks, too, ah, how
3. Mod - ern ways are quite a - larm - ing, Grand - ma says; but boys were

doubt it, How she danced— my grand - ma danced!— Long a -
fun - ny! Real - ly quite a pret - ty girl, Long a -
charm - ing— Girls and boys, I mean, of course— Long a -

go, ____ Long a - go. ____ How she held her pret - ty head, How her
go, ____ Long a - go. ____ Bless her! why, she wears a cap, Grand - ma
go, ____ Long a - go. ____ Brave but mod - est, grand - ly shy She would

dain - ty skirt she spread, ____ Turn - ing out her lit - tle toes; How she
does, and takes a nap ____ Ev - 'ry sin - gle day; and yet Grand - ma
like to have us try ____ Just to feel like those who met In the

slow - ly leaned and rose ____ Long a - go, ____
danced the min - u - et ____ Long a - go, ____
grace - ful min - u - et ____ Long a - go, ____

Long a - go. ____
Long a - go. ____
Long a - go. ____

MY DAFFODILS

Fred G. Bowles

W. Berwald

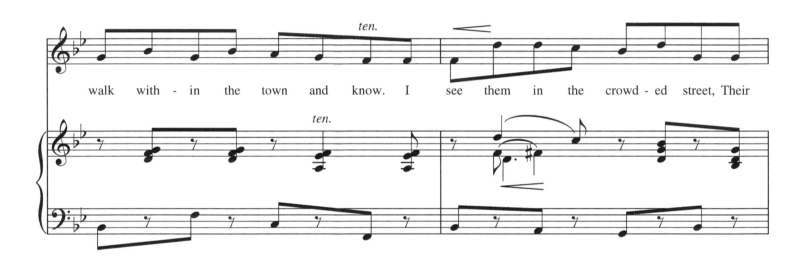

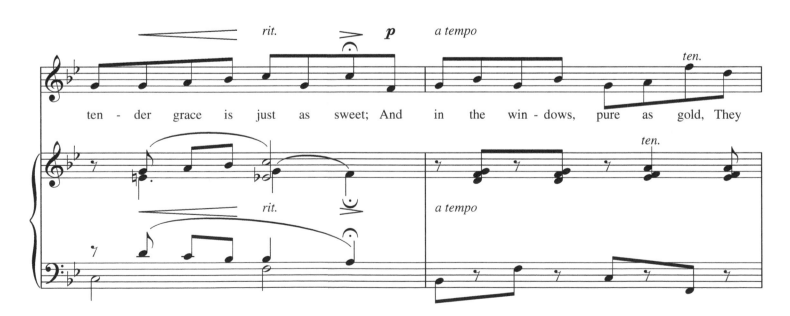

NURSERY RHYMES

Music and Words by
Pearl G. Curran

Hey! did - dle did - dle, The cat and the fid - dle, And the cow jump - ing ov - er the moon; How the lit - tle dog laugh'd with glee, He had nev - er seen such sport, you see. And now, as I re - call, That real - ly was - n't all, For the dish ran a - way with the spoon! The

dish ran a - way with the spoon!

accel. molto

Ped. Ped.

mf

a tempo

f

mf

And old Moth - er Hub - bard, She went to the cup - board, To

get her poor dog a bone; But when she got there The

patetico

cup - board was bare, And so the poor dog - gie had none. _____ And

colla voce

f

Andante

tuck you in from the cold, And we'll sing a lit - tle lul - la - by:

l.h.

Bye - low,— Ba - by - Bye, Yes, I know a lot more Rhymes That we'll

pp

keep for oth - er times, And we'll take a lit - tle nap, you and I, We'll

Ped.

rall.

take a lit - tle nap, you and I.

rallent.

morendo

Ped. *Ped.* *✳*

THE SECRET

Music and Words by
Oley Speaks

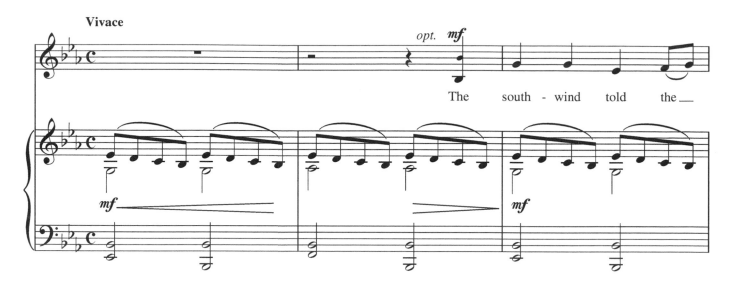

TO MY FIRST LOVE

Edwin Hamilton

Hermann Löhr

I re - mem - ber meet - ing you In Sep - tem - ber Six - ty -

two; We were eat - ing, both of us, ___ And the meet - ing hap - pen'd

thus; Ac - ci - den - tal, on the road, (Sen - ti - men - tal ep - i -

'TIS SPRING

Montrose J. Moses

Harriet Ware

THE WIND

Carolyn S. Bailey

Charles Gilbert Spross

The wild lit-tle Wind fell

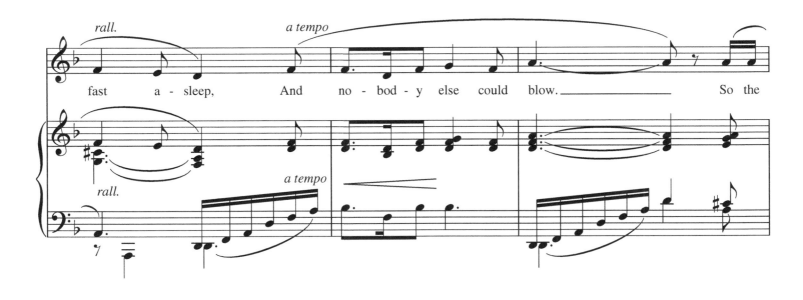

fast a-sleep, And no-bod-y else could blow._____ So the

trees stood tall, and nev-er moved, And the lit-tle leaves missed him

so._____ The lit - tle brown hare for - got to run, The blue - jay for - got to

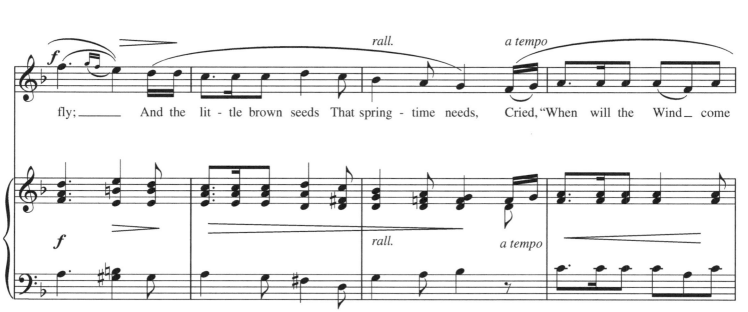

fly;_____ And the lit - tle brown seeds That spring - time needs, Cried, "When will the Wind__ come

by,_____ When will the Wind come by?"_____ The

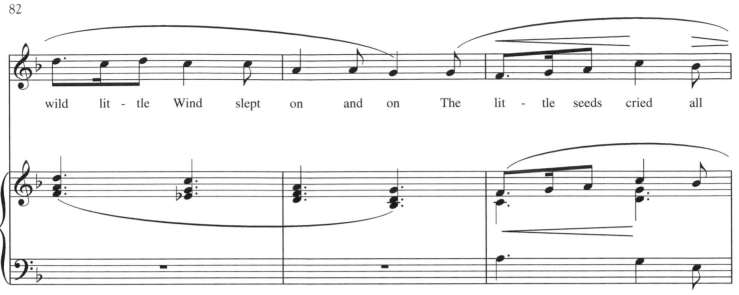

wild lit - tle Wind slept on and on The lit - tle seeds cried all

Tempo I (Allegro)

day,_____ Till a kind old squir - rel picked them up, And car - ried them far a-

rall.

way _____ To the place where lit - tle seeds want to go, And he plant - ed them ev - 'ry

So the wild lit-tle Wind woke up to find That all of his work was done, That all of his work was done.

YOU'D BETTER ASK ME

Samuel Lover

Hermann Löhr

ceiv - ers,   And nev - er, I know will con - sent.____ She says, girls in a hur - ry who

mar - ry,   At lei - sure re - pent."_____

colla voce

Then sup - pose I would talk to your fa - ther, sweet Ma - ry, says I._____ "Oh! don't

talk to my fa - ther, says Ma - ry, be - gin - ning to cry;_____ For my fa - ther he loves me so

VIOLETS

Music and Words by
R. Huntington Woodman